Praise for

COURAGE TO THRIVE

This book is intimate, powerful, and full of faith and hope. Robert Flanagan weaves together his experience, with a theological depth and a spiritual hope, in a way that creates a beautiful and compelling tapestry. In a time when mental illness cripples many a human life, this is a book that might literally save a life. Written with erudition, precision, and love, this is a remarkable set of devotions.

—Ian Markham
Dean of Virginia Theological Seminary

Robert Flanagan not only writes about courage but also exemplifies it. These daily meditations and prayers, candidly offered in his first-person voice, are a heartening accompaniment toward thriving and wholeness.

—Anne Silver
Director, Center for Christian Spirituality at the General Theological Seminary

Reading this book is itself a healing experience. With great personal vulnerability, Bob Flanagan invites us onto a journey into spiritually illuminated psychological health. With lucidity, warmth, and gentleness, we are shown that God loves us in our struggles and can transform them into fullness of life.

—Charles Mayer
Priest and Psychotherapist

D1598590

These meditations plant a seed of peace in the heart of the reader. And don't we all need an extra dose of peace these days? Without shying away from the depth of human suffering, Bob Flanagan offers wise and gentle words of hope. These meditations reveal a deep knowledge of Christian spirituality and unveil how love exceeds our sorrows and fears. This book offers soul-soothing balm for weary hearts.

—Donyelle McCray
Assistant Professor of Homiletics, Yale Divinity School

Rev. Bob Flanagan writes simply and elegantly of his struggle with depression in *Courage to Thrive*. He asks what to do when the helper needs help, then answers the question powerfully and practically. His journey, like so many others, was dark and difficult. Bob outlines his steps to recovery, then offers a series of reflections and prayers. Each shows us how he traveled out of his personal darkness to light and hope. I am not one of great faith, yet I could read these prayers again—they map self-care, reflection, and peace. The helper shares the hope we all need to thrive.

—Nancy Farrell
AFSP National Board Member
and the loss survivor of her brother, Michael

COURAGE
TO THRIVE

Robert D. Flanagan

COURAGE
TO THRIVE

FINDING
Joy and Hope
IN THE MIDST OF
Mental Health
Struggles

Published by Redemption Press, PO Box 427, Enumclaw, WA 98022.

Toll-Free (844) 2REDEEM (273-3336)

Redemption Press is honored to present this title in partnership with the author. The views expressed or implied in this work are those of the author. Redemption Press provides our imprint seal representing design excellence, creative content, and high-quality production.

Scripture quotations marked NRSV are taken from the New Revised Standard Version Bible, copyright © 1989 the Division of Christian Education of the National Council of the Churches of Christ in the United States of America. Used by permission. All rights reserved.

ISBN: 978-1-64645-177-7 (Paperback)
978-1-64645-178-4 (ePub)
978-1-64645-179-1 (Mobi)

Library of Congress Catalog Card Number: 2020911319

CONTENTS

Foreword ix

Introduction 13

1. Acceptance 19

2. Courage 22

3. I Am Loved 25

4. Focus 28

5. Panic Attack 31

6. Sadness 35

7. I Am Sorry 38

8. Fatigue 42

9. Suicidal Ideation 45

10. Dread 49

11. Shame 53

12. Taking Meds 56

13. Just Get Through 60

14. Coping 64

15. Personal Boundaries 68

16. Self-Confidence 72

17. Rest 75

18. Sabbath 79

19. Sleep 82

20. Silence 86

21. Asking for Help 89

22. Vulnerable 92

23. Forgiveness 96

24. Self-Care 100

25. Self-Kindness 104

26. Self-Gentleness 107

27. Humility 111

28. Vulnerability 114

29. Angels 118

30. Worthiness 122

31. Wisdom 125

32. Gratefulness 129

33. Letting Go 132

34. Strength 136

35. Love, Live, and God 139

36. Patience 143

37. Joy 147

38. Peace 150

39. Hope 154

40. Thrive 157

Acknowledgments 161

Notes 163

FOREWORD

Ⅰ N THIS INSPIRING SPIRITUAL JOURNAL, Bob Flanagan provides a unique blend of intimately personal insights grounded in scripturally based spiritual wisdom. His stories are moving, deeply personal, and at times hilarious. A true pioneer and seasoned priest, Bob shares from his own experiences, many based in his mental health experience. This personal narrative boldly delves into the life of the mind as well as of the soul, living with the ebb and flow of depression and anxiety, and it thus affords a whole new window into how mind, body, and soul interrelate, each part of our being affecting the other.

The vast majority of people have experienced mental health challenges at some point in their lives or have interacted with someone who has struggled with their mental health. Yet most of society goes about their daily lives with their attention directed elsewhere, and talking about our mental health often takes a backseat to other topics that appear more pressing. While these can be difficult conversations to have with one another, they are often necessary for many critical steps that can follow. By reflecting on our own patterns of thoughts and behaviors, we learn more about ourselves. We are able to shed the layers of denial and defensiveness that prop up unhealthy ways. Sharing with others also helps us to reach out for help when needed. Mental health struggles can affect us physically, psychologically, relationally, and spiritually. Because of this, these struggles can also be addressed and supported through these same areas.

The truth is that human suffering, angst, and suicidal thoughts are all throughout the Scriptures. Mental health may be a modern concept based in the twentieth-century emergence of neuroscience, psychological studies, and cognitive science, but the human experience of mental health has been with us from the beginning. To no fault of our own, mental health frequently suffers, creating pain, disability, and family suffering. Mental health conditions almost always stem from combined factors as far-reaching as our genetic makeup, early and current experiences, or trauma. Nature and nurture both matter with regard to almost all types of health issues, and mental health is no different.

What is different is the lack of knowledge and the stigma that has shrouded mental health experiences and kept people suffering in silence for millennia. This history of stigma has also kept families, spouses, and loved ones stymied, unsure how to interpret their depressed loved one's behavior, let alone how to support them and find effective treatment and solutions. Society, schools, and workplaces have often discriminated against people with mental health conditions, assuming that behavior is simply a matter of will, requiring discipline, and this has added more layers of suffering, negative self-image, and disability on top of the often disabling symptoms of these health conditions. Looking at biblical Scriptures through this lens allows us to see the many instances of depression, hopelessness, despair, disability, and suicidal impulses that are present, with healing, support, and unconditional love always paired with these experiences.

This book gives individuals a guide to contemplate and connect with their mental health as part of taking care of their well-being and deepening their spiritual existence. Through Bob's honest disclosure and wise devotions, we see both his faith and his struggles, and they coexist to inform us. He addresses an often-neglect-ed truth of our human experience—that our struggles provide us with the opportunity for emotional and spiritual growth if we allow them. This important aspect of our human experience allows us also to connect with others who struggle. Bob's vulnerability allows us to acknowledge the good that can come when we open ourselves up to sharing our struggles, both with other people and in our spiritual life.

Christine Moutier, MD, Chief Medical Officer
Doreen Marshall, PhD, VP of Mission Engagement
American Foundation for Suicide Prevention

INTRODUCTION

*In the middle of the journey of our life, I came to
myself in a dark wood, for the straight way was lost.*
—Inferno

I PREACHED ABOUT MY EXPERIENCE with suicidal thoughts when
I had been a first-year seminarian some twenty years earlier. The
sermon was a kick-in-the-ass message meant to remind the seminary students of the extraordinary work God called them to do
and to stop complaining about their workload. A tall, thoughtful
dark-haired student named Mike approached me after the service.
He said that I had a lot of courage to share my mental health issues. I didn't want the sermon to be about me—I never do—so
I hoped my personal story hadn't overshadowed my comments
about priesthood or God. Yet I felt compelled to share the message
that a seminary student and priest could have a mental illness and
still thrive.

When I was thirty-seven, about the same age as Dante
Alighieri's character in the poem *Inferno*, I found myself lost "in
a dark wood." His narrator describes it as a place "so savage and
harsh and strong that the thought of it renews my fears."[1] I don't
disagree, and as with the narrator, I didn't know how I got there or
the way out.

In his memoir *Darkness Visible*, William Styron, the author of
Sophie's Choice, used Dante's dark wood to describe the "fathomless
ordeal" of depression and the "ravages of melancholia."[2] I would

go further than Styron and include anxiety, panic attacks, and thoughts of suicide in that dark wood as well.

Since I'm a priest, you shouldn't be surprised to learn that my way out of that place was a spiritual journey. On the other hand, you may be surprised that a priest, a person who claims a close relationship with God and who has been affirmed by the church, has suffered from depression, anxiety, panic attacks, and suicidal thoughts. Ha! I say. I am human. Besides, if you have ever read the book in the Bible called Psalms, you would know that the struggle with mental health is a central theme. Let me also state I'm not crazy. Those four illnesses meant my brain was not well and I needed help. I would even say that my mental illness has made me a more compassionate pastor, preacher, and priest.

To leave the dark wood of mental illness takes courage. When I preached to the faculty and students at the General Theological Seminary in 2019 about my mental illness, I had to be courageous. Still, it was a scant amount when compared to the courage I needed during the first days in the dark wood. From its beginning to end, the journey of mental illness can only be undertaken with courage.

Styron quoted the last lines of *Inferno* at the end of his memoir: "And thence we came forth to look again at the stars."[3] He likened his return to mental health with Dante's exit from hell. But, dearest reader, that is not enough. I am not content with emerging from darkness to stargaze. I want more, and so do you. I want to thrive.

In *The Anatomy of Courage*, Lord Moran analyzed the psychological effects of war on World War I soldiers to understand the difference between courage and fear. At its core, he wrote, "Courage is a moral quality. It is a cold choice between two alternatives, the fixed resolve not to quit. An act of renunciation which must be made not once but many times by the power of the will. Courage is will power."[4]

When our brain is ill, we must decide to get out of bed every day and keep going until we can thrive. In either the chaos of the battlefield or the stillness of a bedroom, people need the same courage. But unlike the battlefield, no one will call us a coward if we never emerge from the depths of depression, anxiety, panic attacks, or suicidal thoughts. They will grimly nod at us or, worse, tell us to get over it, as if pain and suffering of the brain are imaginary. In the battle for mental health, we also don't share foxholes with others—the journey is ours alone.

To thrive, we must take the right steps. To be courageous, Moran wisely states, "We must acknowledge that there is but one thing to do, then we shall go and do it."[5] In my experience, I needed the courage to carry out four vital steps.

I first had to accept that I was sick. At the onset, I could convince myself that I was okay. It's a curious thing to be mentally ill but think you're healthy. Of course, I wasn't, but I could accomplish enough to make do.

I then had to be willing to keep meeting with my doctors and therapists. I couldn't simply pop a pill and be better. The medicine had to be adjusted and conversations had to happen before I started to feel better. Still, I also hit setbacks when I needed new drugs, different dosages, or new therapists and doctors to talk with. The medical part takes grit not to give up, and it's easy to get frustrated and scared and to walk away.

I had to be persistent. I had good days and bad days, good weeks and bad weeks. I would feel great for a couple of days or even a week. Something would happen, and I would spiral back into a dense copse filled with ancient trees and bramble with long thorns. What then to do? I had to repeat steps one and two. I begrudgingly admitted I was still sick, and I had to work with my doctor and therapist to unlock more memories of trauma. Trust me—if I could have gotten healthy through persistent, bold, heartfelt prayer, I would have won a trophy. Prayer helped, but for me, it wasn't the answer. Each day I had to be persistent and keep at it.

The final step is time. I don't like to say that because the thought makes me weary. We live in an age of speed and instant gratification, but part of what made me better was time. Since the brain is a complex organ, I needed to sit patiently with my thoughts and re-examine my memories. It was like solving a jigsaw puzzle or cleaning up a room after a kid's birthday party. My brain was a mess, and restoring order and cleanliness couldn't be rushed or ignored.

Each step requires courage. I didn't then and still don't enjoy examining my feelings and emotions. I'm a guy, after all, and ignoring mental illness is not limited to men (cis-males). Really, it isn't. I needed lots of courage to look at my painful experiences of abuse and trauma. However, as Moran writes, "Courage is expendable."[6] Even the best soldier needs a break from the action or to come off the line, as it were. The journey from the dark wood to a place of thriving cannot be completed without rest. I didn't like to admit it, but I had to stop from time to time. One reason, as Moran notes, is that fear "feeds on the memory of things,"[7] and fear depletes courage. Without courage to face what causes anxiety and such, we can't overcome fear. Many days I felt as if I were untying several of my daughter's necklaces that were jumbled together, and it was frustrating and frightening. Courage, memory, fear, and anxiety can be knotted together. It is a dark wood.

The journey is worth it. To thrive is to live in joy, peace, and hope. It isn't about fame or money. Maybe you want something more grandiose, but let's face it, if you have joy, peace, and hope, what else matters? Joy is a state of being that flows from the soul. When joy is tapped into, it will wash over us as nothing else can. Peace is a gift from God. We can only receive that gift if we acknowledge God and open our hearts to him. With the peace of God, little can upset us. Hope is what feeds the peace of God and is the ultimate quality of thriving. When I imagined living without anxiety, depression, panic attacks, or suicidal thoughts, I became hopeful and drawn to a positive, light-filled future. I could relax and smile, knowing my cares may weigh me down but they will pass.

I've written this book so you may see that thriving is possible. I hope my journey can be a beacon for you. I want you to be inspired and excited, knowing the reflections I have written are meant to mirror your experiences and motivate you to thrive. If a priest can have a mental illness, then you're not alone. If I can get frustrated and disappointed with the fight through the dark wood, then you can feel that way too. Journey with me for the next forty days. Please don't rush through the book in one sitting. You'll miss the point. And read the prayer at the end of each reflection, knowing I wrote it from my experience as a gift for you. Drink the words I've shared with you, especially the prayers, and "let anyone who wishes take the water of life as a gift" (Revelation 22:17).

one

ACCEPTANCE ✨

Who has put wisdom in the inward parts, or given
understanding to the mind?
Job 38:36

I ALWAYS THOUGHT OF MYSELF as a calm, well-adjusted, confident person, but that's a lie. Maybe not a lie, but it's not entirely true. When I saw my doctor write his diagnosis at the bottom of a page with my name at the top, I was confused. He wrote that so the insurance company would pay my claim, didn't he? Because that is not me, or not the real me. I'm a dad, a husband, and a priest. Did I really have depression and anxiety?

I won't call that time in my life (my late thirties and forties) my Dark Night, because I've read the poem with that title by the Spanish mystic John of the Cross. I like the poem and the dark nights. But I was taking medication for anxiety and depression. I don't want to think about it, but I was depressed and do suffer from anxiety. Many nights I would dream about having an anxiety attack only to wake with my heart pounding and accelerating, as if it were a race car surging off the starting line.

I'm in a better place now. I feel like the barred owl, with its face of wisdom, that called out last night. It's one of those dark-night friends. The owl's hoot reminds me that while the world is quiet, it's not asleep. While I rest, if my dreams let me, the creatures of the night live. We each have our part, our role to play in God's world. I don't understand it all, nor am I meant to. I have, however, learned that my brain can be sick or unwell, and through it all, I'm still loved by God. At times I still struggle to accept the illness and the severe difficulties it causes me.

Prayer

My Lord and my God, you glittered the night sky with stars and filled the dark depths of the ocean with life. Assist me to accept the ways of the world and my place in it; help me understand my brain and its complexities; comfort me when my mind is agitated and anxious; and support me when I am weak. In Jesus's name I pray. Amen.

Prompt

How would accepting your mental health struggles change you?

_____

_____

_____

_____

_____

_____

two

COURAGE

Be strong and courageous; do not be frightened or
dismayed, for the Lord your God is with you
wherever you go.
Joshua 1:9

I HAD JUST FINISHED EXPLAINING the situation to my therapist—
yes, a priest needs therapy. He calmly said that I was courageous.
Someone else had said that of me before, but when he said it, I let it
sink in and wondered if my therapist was right. To me, soldiers and
first responders are courageous. My life is entirely safe and secure,
not risky or perilous.

I wrestled with what he said for a time and decided how I have
been courageous. When I was living with depression and chose to
get out of bed, that was an act of courage. The mornings after I
experienced a nighttime anxiety attack and went to my seminary
classes or work, I was heroic. It took guts to come home from an
exhausting, emotional day and focus on my wife and kids. So I
have countless acts of courage in my life. They are the times when

I chose to step toward the light and not remain in the darkness of fear.

I don't always feel God's presence with me, and I suppose the Israelite leader Joshua, who took over after Moses died, didn't either. But I trust God is with me wherever I go. I believe in God just like I think getting out of bed, going to work, or being with my family is an act of faith. When the darkness sought to surround me and almost consumed me, I found the courage to live.

Maybe you have had those days when simply putting your feet on the floor is an accomplishment. I want you to know it's more than that. It's courage. No less than an emergency worker responding to a call, choosing to live takes determination and fortitude. You are a hero because you choose light, love, and life.

Prayer

Blessed and Gracious God, you light the world and give me life. Forgive my moments of weaknesses and cowardice; grant me the courage to live; fill me with the blessing of your love; and keep watch over me, so I don't fall into the abyss of darkness or the pit of fear and despair. I am nothing without you, and you're my hope. Amen.

Prompt

When have you been courageous?

_____

_____

_____

_____

_____

three

I AM LOVED

My beloved is mine and I am his.
Song of Solomon 2:16

WHEN I AM AT PEACE and let my mind go, I feel connected not just to creation but to the abiding love of God that weaves its threads through it all. The love is there in the depth of despair, the darkness brought upon me when others diminish me, and the loneliness caused when people fail to sense my sadness. We humans fail each other, sometimes miserably, but God doesn't. God's love doesn't remove the pain or make the hurt vanish, but instead I know I am not alone and never will be. I am always loved.

The fourteenth-century English anchorite Julian of Norwich knew this love. In the sixty-first chapter of *Showings*, she wrote, "And by the experience of this falling we shall have a great and marvelous knowledge of love in God without end; for enduring and marvelous is that love which cannot and will not be broken because of offenses."[8] While her sense of "falling" pointed toward sin, the love of which she spoke is the same love that connects us to all things and God. She added, "Mother Jesus may never suffer us who are his children to perish, for he is almighty, all wisdom and all love, and so is none but he, blessed may he be."[9]

Julian enjoyed imagining Jesus as a mother and lover. She was not heretical or insincere but open to every type of love we can feel. Her wisdom shows us that divine love is all and complete. Whether we fail others or God or if others harm or fail us, we ever and always have God's love.

When so many people let us down, and we hurt so many, our world can seem awful. Despite the misery and chaos that never seems far away, I feel loved. From this, I find hope, which lets me love others. Although my heart has been scarred and broken over the years, I can open my heart to others because it's filled with God's love.

Prayer

Sweet God of love and source of all light, you are marvelous and beloved to me. Hold me in your arms of mercy, kiss me with your lips of grace, wrap me in your charity, and let me feel the comfort of your strength. Protect me from the misery and chaos that presses near me; be close to me when I am lonely; relieve the pain of despair; support me when others won't; forgive me when I fail those I love and you. I live forever in your love. Amen.

Prompt

If you could imagine yourself held in God's arms, what would that be like?

_____

_____

_____

four

FOCUS

Let your eyes look directly forward,
and your gaze be straight before you.
Proverbs 4:25

I N *THE ASCENT OF MOUNT Carmel,* the Spanish mystic John of
the Cross emphasizes the importance of spiritual emptiness. He
states that faith is "infused and rooted more deeply in the soul
by means of emptiness" toward all things.[10] By letting go of everything—desires and worries—one can connect more deeply to
God. In this state of desolation, the soul increases in faith, love,
and hope.

I appreciate John of the Cross's advice, but he wouldn't get
me. When my anxiety kicks in, I struggle to focus because I often
have ten thoughts swirling around my mind all at once. I wish I
could think of nothing or just one thing. My brain becomes overwhelmed with feeling, and I worry my mind will freeze up and
stop. If I could turn it off and on, like a computer, that might help.
When my thoughts race, stopping them is tough, nearly impossi-

ble. I can't meditate or pray because thoughts crowd my attention. I struggle to get anything done and usually make mistakes. Forget about doing math! My focus is shot.

Only one thing works—I need to give in and let each thought come to the foreground. It's often something I fear or am worried about. I then hold my hand over my heart and gently affirm the emotion associated with it. I let myself feel, saying I have room for the feeling. After I finish, the thought's intensity and emotion lessen. I repeat it, giving space to all of them. I'm always surprised that I have room for all my feelings. Only then can I let my eyes look directly ahead and find that spiritual emptiness where silence and peace unfold.

Prayer

O God, mighty ruler and gentle comforter, assuage my thoughts. Grant me the courage to feel the smallest and greatest emotions within me; allow them to come forth one at a time and not over-whelm me; let me accept each feeling for what it is; and then assist me to find peaceful, silent emptiness in my mind, body, and soul. Amen.

Prompt

If you felt confident that your emotions would not overwhelm you, what feelings would you let emerge?

_____

_____

_____

_____

_____

_____

_____

_____

_____

_____

_____

_____

_____

_____

_____

_____

_____

_____

_____

_____

_____

_____

_____

_____

five

PANIC ATTACK

I am utterly spent and crushed;
I groan because of the tumult of my heart.
Psalm 32:8

THE PREVIOUS NIGHT, A STRANGE feeling kept waking me. I was worried about moving to seminary: shuttering my business, relocating hundreds of miles, separating my wife from her family and friends, and taking our kids from their familiar school and friends. But the next morning I followed my usual routine, getting myself out the door after helping with the kids. I thought I was okay.

The sky was gray and unremarkable as I sped down the interstate a few miles to my first appointment. I began to shake, and a groan emerged from deep inside me. My heart rapidly accelerated until my whole body shook. The sensation came in waves. I quickly exited, awkwardly pulling over at the bottom of the ramp. My hands trembled as another wave overflowed from within.

I thought about getting out of my car but felt sure I would

collapse and die if I did. Instead I slowly drove to the hospital. Stupid, I know. When I walked into the emergency department, they took me right in. I looked that bad. When my doctor came into the room, I cried, and then my heartbeat slowed. Not the typical symptoms of a heart attack, he said.

The force of mental illness can crush us, and fear can utterly deplete us. The tumult of the heart is real. The psalmist's words remind us that we're not alone, but panic is lonely these days. I have rarely spoken about what happened to me. I received help from doctors and therapists. But what friend or family member—certainly not the bishop—could understand my fear and panic? I took the meds, talked with counselors, and prayed a lot. All of which helped, and so did time. I needed time to live and see that everything would work out for the best.

In the twenty-seventh chapter of *Revelation of Divine Love*, the fourteenth-century English mystic Julian of Norwich wrote, "All will be well, and all will be well, and every kind of thing shall be well."[11] She lived through the black plague. She knew.

Prayer

You are my God, whom I fear and love, but sometimes I am overwhelmed, and my body rebels against me. During these times, my body frightens me, and I desperately want the adrenaline to stop. I cry out to you, but the suffering doesn't end. I call upon you, and you are near. I am safe, but my mind doesn't believe it. What am I missing? I need to be well. Help me, dear God. I feel lost. Amen.

Prompt

How would your life be different if you felt God's safety when your body frightens you?

six

SADNESS

And he said to them, "What are you discussing
with each other while you walk along?"
They stood still, looking sad.
Luke 24:17

As I recovered from my depression, once again I started to recognize my feelings. For example, when I was sad but not depressed. When I felt unusually sad one day, I called a mentor and left a message I was feeling sad but otherwise okay. I felt good even though I was sad. I wasn't afraid either, because I understood the sadness would soon pass.

My mentor called me back and, rather unempathetically, announced I should talk to a therapist. I thanked him and replied that I was okay. I wanted someone to know how I felt, but I could sense his fear. Afterward, I chuckled, though his response miffed me. He's a priest, after all, and had reacted as if he'd touched a hot stove.

The verse above from Luke is from an encounter two of Jesus's followers had with a stranger on the road to Emmaus. Unbeknown to them, the stranger was the resurrected Jesus. Unlike my mentor, Jesus reacted not with fear or aversion to their sadness but inquired what was wrong. They recounted Jesus's death and the perplexing and frightening empty tomb. Jesus listened, and they felt heard, easing their sadness.

Sadness occurs naturally. We can embrace and welcome it. If it lasts more than a few days, then we should be concerned. John of the Cross notes, "Sadness makes people open their eyes and see the advantage or harm in things."[12] He wisely states that through sadness, we can make sense of our situations and ourselves, often better than when we're happy. Sorrow can bring inquiry and wisdom. It's not meant to scare us; instead it is an important emotion.

Prayer

Generous and gentle God, you have enriched me with innumerable emotions and feelings. Encourage me to sense and accept all my feelings. When I am sad, let me not worry or fear that it will consume me but rather strengthen me to wade into the sadness. May I see it as a place of growth and a source of wisdom. Let me dwell in the waters for a short time and emerge refreshed and wrapped in your love. In Jesus's name I pray. Amen.

Prompt

Think of a time when you were sad. What caused it? How did you react?

_____

_____

_____

seven

I AM SORRY

I confess my iniquity; I am sorry for my sin.
Psalm 38:18

I USED TO SAY "I'M sorry" a lot. When I misspoke in public, I would say it. If I bumped into someone, I apologized. When I was late or interrupted someone, I repeated it. I do it less these days and am more careful about my apologies. I've changed my thinking.

For starters, I used to think I didn't matter. Well, I mattered, but not that much. When I felt I was imposing on someone, I would apologize. I think back on those days and cringe but also get why I was doing it. I thought people would be nicer to me if I apologized, even when I didn't have to. I recognize now that an unwarranted apology is annoying. I still need to bite my tongue, stopping myself from doing it, but I've changed.

I know I matter now, even when others don't care or think I matter. That's their problem. For instance, the other day I was out for a run on a beautiful trail along a river. Walkers, some with dogs, also frequent it. Two things happened. I initially encountered two people with a dog that should have been on a leash but wasn't, right? The big black dog barked incessantly, demanding a stick to be thrown. When I was maybe ten feet behind them, one swung a four-foot stick behind her without first looking. She nearly threw the stick at me, and only at the last moment did she adjust her throw to miss me. I grimaced and continued. Later, I encountered a couple walking side by side, which left no room for anyone else to pass. I came up from behind and announced my presence with "excuse me," which sounded like "move over and share the trail, idiot," but in the politest way!

Now that I know I matter, I don't apologize for the error of others. The person should have looked before starting to throw a stick, and the couple should have been more sensitive to the presence of others. Neither instance was my fault, and I too had every right to be there. No apologies needed. You and I have every right to be in the world.

Prayer

Dearest Lord and creator of all, I sometimes feel as if I don't matter, but you value all of creation, even me. Encourage me to find my place in the world and courageously claim it. Let me see where I make mistakes, but prohibit me from claiming the mistakes of others as my own. Strengthen me to walk shoulder to shoulder with all people, and grant me the confidence to do so without hesitation. Amen.

Prompt

Think of a time when you apologized for someone else's mistake. What made you do that, and how did you feel?

eight

FATIGUE

Come to me, all you that are weary and are carrying
heavy burdens, and I will give you rest.
Matthew 11:28

I WAS DRIVING HOME ONE afternoon and saw a neighbor out for
a walk. When I passed her, I noticed that she looked exhausted.
After parking the car, I called out to her and asked how she was.
She said, "Okay," and started to come closer. We met at the end
of my driveway. She had that familiar look of fatigue, as if she had
spent the day slogging through bitter water. We caught up on life
and spoke about our anxieties.

What is it about anxiety that depletes us? Some days I over-
flow with energy, but the next day I can be fatigued and lethargic.
Life with anxiety is often more draining than I expect. That is why
Jesus's invitation is so appealing. I do get weary and tire from carrying heavy burdens, even if others think it's all in my head. My
head can be heavy. So cut me some slack. When I'm at my limit,
I imagine Jesus carrying some or all my burdens, those cares and

concerns about life that overwhelm me. With Jesus's help, I can make it through my day and even smile.

I want to smile, laugh, and enjoy life—to thrive. I can't do that if I haul all my concerns around. I want some help—wouldn't you? Talking with a friend is helpful, no doubt. But for me, closing my eyes and handing a box of worries to Jesus is more effective. I can return to Jesus anytime to root around my box of cares and concerns, finding the ones that need attention. That's freedom. When I am unburdened, I can rest and find my center again. Imagine drifting off to sleep after you handed off that box for the night. Peaceful, right? It is for me.

Prayer

Lord Jesus, my strength and salvation, come to my aid. I have no energy and struggle to live. I need you to take from me my worries and cares, even just for a time. Support me while life presses around me and all others have deserted me. I want to thrive but can only do so with your helping hand. Give me the rest that you promise to all who draw near to you. Amen.

Prompt

How would it feel if Jesus carried your burdens today? What difference would it make?

_____

_____

_____

_____

_____

nine

SUICIDAL IDEATION

*When the jailer woke up and saw the prison doors
wide open, he drew his sword and was about to
kill himself, since he supposed that the prisoners
had escaped.*
Acts of the Apostles 16:27

THE IMAGE THAT BEST DESCRIBES my thoughts of suicide is holding the end of a frayed rope. I can only see the rope because darkness surrounds it. I want to let go but don't. The image captures the way I felt when I was in crisis during that October day in seminary. It's like the jailer's crisis, waking up after an earthquake and seeing the prison doors wide open. The jailer was lucky the apostle Paul was there to stop him. I had to find my way through the fear on my own.

No one reason can explain suicidal ideation. It is a complex and perplexing illness of the brain. The experience involves both the most rational irrational and the most irrational rational of thinking, which makes sense and no sense at the same time. The best response is to seek help and let the thoughts be, giving them no value. Researchers say the suicidal crisis passes quickly, in less than an hour, maybe as soon as thirty-five minutes. It would have helped to know these facts back then. I could have shaken off some of the fear gripping my mind: my fear of death, of my mental illness, and of failing to become a priest.

Another fact would have been helpful—I'm not the only one to have felt the urge to end my life, and neither are you. Many people have thoughts of suicide each year. Thankfully, most never act on them. What's important to recognize is that such thoughts are signs of a brain in crisis and the need to seek medical help. Keep this phone number, 800-273-8255, to the National Suicide Prevention Lifeline. Someone is available 24/7 to talk things through and help.

Suicidal ideation profoundly changed my life. For a long time it frightened me, but not now. I remain cautious and wary. I have volunteered with the American Foundation for Suicide Prevention since 2010, helping in a variety of ways. My work has shown me that suicidal thoughts are symptoms of an illness, not much different than any other serious illness.

Prayer

God of greatness and majesty, you have made me fragile and precious. I need your protection from the thoughts that frighten me. Come to my aid, for I'm overwhelmed, and the darkness is near. I fear that my grip is slipping. Hold me close and carry me through my desperate times. I cast my hope on you alone, so guide me to safety. Amen.

Prompt

What thoughts frighten you?

_____

_____

_____

_____

_____

_____

_____

_____

_____

_____

_____

_____

_____

_____

_____

_____

_____

_____

ten

DREAD

*I am poured out like water, and all my bones are out
of joint; my heart is like wax; it is melted within
my breast; my mouth is dried up like a potsherd,
and my tongue sticks to my jaws; you lay me in the
dust of death.*
Psalm 22:14–15

I HAD MY FIRST PANIC attack before arriving at my seminary but
didn't understand what dread felt like until after I had started
my fall classes. I would wake in the night, feeling as if the world
was closing in on me. My limbs would grow cold, and my heartbeat would quicken. I would often have a sudden urge to go to the
bathroom. I then would sit in bed, believing my life would end.

I'm glad the psalmist dared to write so honestly and openly
about his feelings. During the days when panic attacks would rav-
age my body, I took comfort knowing that a biblical writer had felt
the same way I did. The words and their meaning consoled me. I
wasn't the only one to have experienced panic, and I relied on his
faith to see me through.

Panic attacks have an annihilating element to them. I often felt as if I were at the edge of eternal darkness. One slip and I would fall in, never to see the light again. Not that I cared, or at least part of me didn't care. Another part of me would cry to God. When the dread took hold, I battled between the opposing forces of annihilation and existence. I was a tiny boat riding the foam and froth of a boiling ocean.

In those moments, my mind and body baffled me. I didn't want to experience panic's dread, but some part of me was terrified beyond understanding. I could only cast my care upon God. With the help of meds, the attacks would pass, but I only discovered the root of my fear years later. The fear within me was real, even though the threat was not. I was perfectly safe. Having faith didn't make the dread go away, but it did allow me to carry on, knowing that, like the psalmist, I was not despised by God, and he had heard my cry.

Prayer

Loving and mighty God, whom I love with all my heart and soul, be near me when the terrors of the dark night set upon me. Save me from dread and despair; keep me from slipping into the emptiness and nothingness that feels so close; hold me when my body and brain have abandoned me; and carry me to the safety of morning's light. I need you, dearest Lord. Amen.

Prompt

Imagine you are swimming for shore but are too tired to make it. What would it feel like to have God rescue you and bring you to shore?

eleven

SHAME

In you, O Lord, I take refuge;
let me never be put to shame.
Psalm 71:1

I AM ASHAMED OF A handful of incidents. I don't need to share the specifics, but they are from my childhood, when I was mean, rude, or inappropriate. For many years I forgot them. I shrugged them off as youthful indiscretions. In therapy, I recently recalled a few. As I explored them, I realized the mental weariness they caused me. I'm not the only one who carries shame around as if it's a heavy suitcase. What I failed to recognize is these bags of shame are above the maximum weight limit for mental vibrancy, and it's cost me.

As a priest, I have had plenty of private, confidential conversations with people. On occasion, some speak about their shame. A man told me about his internet pornography addiction and how he struggled to stop. A woman once spoke about the restraining order she put on her husband and how she felt ashamed to have married him. Several have told me about the shame they feel due to mental illness. I find that they, like me, seldom mention their shame to another person. It's simply too much.

The Psalms often speak of shame. In Psalm 71, the author opens his plea to God with it. He wants deliverance from trouble, and in his trust, he hopes that God will not abandon him to his enemies. My enemies are not like the psalmist's, who feels the hand of the wicked near him. Instead my foes are my memories, which are as cruel and unjust. I did things in my youth and, on occasion, as an adult that I wish I could take back: unkind words spoken in anger and the neglect of someone else's need.

While I can't undo the actions, I've spoken about them with my therapist and my wife. When appropriate, I have talked with the person I hurt, and I have brought my shame to God in confession. These steps allow me to unload my unhealthy mental weight and to live in wholeness. I am better for it.

Prayer

O God, you are merciful and gracious, and I fear your judgment and wrath. Hear my plea and cries, for I am ashamed of the things I have done to others, myself, and you. Do not leave me, for my mouth is dry, and the memories of my harmful and inappropriate actions burden me. Open your heart to me and listen to my confessions. Forgive me and restore me to health. Guide me to do the right things now and in the days to come. Amen.

Prompt

What are some things you want to confess to God?

_____

_____

_____

twelve

TAKING MEDS ✒

The Lord created medicines out of the earth,
and the sensible will not despise them.
Ecclesiastes 38:4

YEAH, RIGHT. *DESPISE* MIGHT BE a bit too strong of a feeling, but I didn't want to take anxiety medicine at first. My dirty little secret is, I still don't. Over the last twenty years, I've been taking meds. I've had a couple of breaks. Each lasted a couple of years. But something would happen, and I wound up back on the pills.

I remember when my first doctor wanted to prescribe me an antidepressant. My heart sank. I had been in denial about how much help I needed and my state of mind. I also fretted that the medicine would somehow change me. Really? As if the panic attacks a couple of nights a week and lack of sleep weren't affecting me—would the meds make me different by stabilizing my mood? I can only speak for me, but I am better because of them. I tried a couple of different medicines and dosages to get it right. When I switched, I felt the side effects, but I managed.

Taking meds that affect the brain is a serious business. It's not a job for just any doctor, and the key is an excellent psychiatrist who works with a good therapist. I have an experienced team I trust. They help me see where my old coping skills no longer work and show me new approaches to cope with life's stressors. The brain can be mysterious, and I'm struck that naming what I feel helps so much.

I know the medicine helps and gets me to a better place, along with therapy, but I don't like having to take a pill to function better. That's the stigma talking, right? Many of us live through tough situations that aren't our fault. They just happen. I could cry about mine, which I have, but I would rather live my life. More than that, I want to thrive. So if taking meds lets me do that, then I won't despise them.

Prayer

My Lord and my God, I implore you to spread your mercy on me and increase my trust in my doctors. Reassure me that my pain may be assuaged by the power of medicine, and console my spirit's worry that what I take won't make me worse. Grant me patience as my brain adjusts to the chemicals helping it heal, but also empower me to work with my doctors to find the treatment best for me. If I am not best served by my medical team, encourage me to find a new one. I ask this in the name of the great healer, your Son, Jesus Christ. Amen.

Prompt

What do you fear about taking medication? What questions do you want to ask your doctor but haven't?

_____

_____

_____

_____

_____

_____

_____

_____

_____

_____

_____

_____

_____

_____

_____

_____

_____

_____

_____

thirteen

JUST GET THROUGH

My days are swifter than a weaver's shuttle,
and come to their end without hope.
Job 7:6

I DON'T KNOW ABOUT YOU, but I hate the phrase, "Just get through." In part it suggests that it's okay to suffer or when suffering happens I am supposed to endure it quietly. Dr. Scott Peck's famous opening line from *The Road Less Traveled* is, "Life is difficult."[13] I wouldn't deny that. As a priest, I'm aware everyone faces difficulty—not even money protects one from tragedy, death, and despair. I don't, however, see suffering as something to get through or endure. One might value the lessons learned by suffering after it's over, but in it, hardly. When at all possible, we must alleviate suffering. For all its glorification by some Christians, suffering isn't a good thing.

Even at its worst, life is more than surviving. I might not be able to change my circumstances, but if I were supposed to just get through anxiety and depression, I never would have. Neither would the Hebrew Scripture figure Job, whose biblical account is a story set in ancient times. When we meet him, he is a wealthy, honorable, devout man with a large family. One day calamities strike on all sides, and what follows is a series of interactions with his friends, who want him to "just get through." However, it is God, not his friends, who set Job straight. The account seeks to answer a few questions, including why good and religious people suffer and why good people bother worshiping God. The book also examines the most relevant question for me: In the face of arbitrary suffering, what is the point of life? When the account ends, Job is no longer grieving and depressed but is a better person who became more prosperous.

Immediately after his calamity, Job sits in the dust, mired in misery. After a time, fed up with his friends, who only wanted to fix him, Job becomes angry. He takes his complaints to God, who answers him with a series of questions that leave Job silent, acknowledging his place in the world as a creature made by God. I like that Job complains to God and shows while he might not understand why disaster struck him, he still wanted to live. Job becomes a feisty fighter. He wanted more than "just get through"— he wanted to thrive. Even on my worst days, I want more than to get through. I want to wring every drop of life from each day. I want the same for you.

Prayer

Magnificent God, whose powers are beyond my understanding, in my darkest days, be near me and hear my cries. Do not leave me in grief and despair. Don't merely comfort and console me, but instill in me a desire to live and inspire me to thrive. Amen.

Prompt

If you could, what complaints would you make to God?

_____

_____

_____

_____

_____

_____

_____

_____

_____

_____

_____

_____

_____

_____

_____

_____

_____

_____

fourteen

COPING

*And just then there appeared a woman with a spirit
that had crippled her for eighteen years. She was
bent over and was quite unable to stand up straight.
When Jesus saw her, he called her over and said,
"Woman, you are set free from your ailment."*
Luke 13:11–12

H ER NAME, FAMILY, AND PHYSICAL description didn't matter,
only her gender and disease, a spirit of weakness. One of the
fears I have about talking about my mental illness is that I will be
identified only by the sickness in my brain. None of us want to be
depersonalized or dehumanized by a condition, but our culture
prefers to name people by their troubling diseases. He has cancer.
She has HIV. He's depressed. That one tried to commit suicide, as
if it is a crime, even!

Credit, however, belongs to the bent woman. She was coping with her weakness and didn't stop living her life. On the Sab-

bath, she went to the synagogue, though it likely meant people would whisper about her again. She worshiped God with others in the place that gave her most solace. She faced her illness and the shameful comments head on.

Although these days the word carries a negative undertone, *coping* is an old word with a positive meaning. As a verb, it originally meant "to quarrel," but it grew to mean "to handle successfully."[14] The bent woman dealt with her condition by not letting it stop her from living. When Jesus saw her, he may have recognized her coping and was moved to set her free. That thought strengthens me.

For eighteen years, the woman lived her life despite her weakness. She couldn't look anyone in the eye and yet continued with her daily routines, not seeking help but instead facing her life with courage. She persevered despite the depersonalizing nameless identification made by others.

If I may be a bit preachy, I want to live in a world where people aren't known by their illness, especially a mental health issue. I also recognize we don't live in that world, but with courage by enough of us, one day we will.

Prayer

Merciful and gracious God, who sustains me when I am weak and tired, strengthen me to confront the depersonalizing moments in my day. Give me the firmness to be in public when I feel exposed and compromised by my illness; encourage me to face down those who whisper petty words; and allow me to cope with my infirmities so that I may live well despite them. Amen.

Prompt

If you have been depersonalized, what did it feel like? If you have had to cope with mental illness, what was that like?

fifteen

PERSONAL BOUNDARIES

Keep your heart with all vigilance,
for from it flow the springs of life.
Proverbs 4:23

IN HIS POEM "MENDING WALL," Robert Frost writes, "I let my neighbor know beyond the hill; / And on a day we meet to walk the line / And set the wall between us once again." Later in the poem, the neighbor says, "Good fences make good neighbors."[15] Like fences, personal boundaries make good neighbors, friends, co-workers, and family members. But no matter how much I like clear personal boundaries, I run into people who ignore them, and they drive me nuts.

One guy was notorious for getting under my skin. Within the first hour of my arrival at a new church, unannounced and uninvited he barged into my office. He must have had the deed to the place. He was that aggressive. As we stood in the middle of my office—I wasn't going to let him sit—he purposely stepped into my personal space, getting within two feet of me. He informed me he was the head of a particular church group. Of course, no one else had mentioned that, which I told him. Not that it mattered—he was there to measure me up by violating my personal boundaries. It was a power play, no question. In my work, people often play for power. Yeah, I know—it's the church. That's not supposed to happen.

People who violate my personal boundaries agitate me. I get annoyed, frustrated, angry, and dismayed. At its worst, my anxiety kicks in, compounding it all. I do my best to stay calm, but sometimes I can't, and my anger boils. Yes, I'm a priest, but I don't have to be nice all the time, do I? I am human. It's funny how I must remind people of that.

When I get into it with a boundary violator, I handle him or her with "I" statements. First, I must have a clear understanding of what I want in the relationship, but once I do, I speak from where I am, how I feel, and what I want. Doing so lowers my anxiety to a point where I can function. With some people, that's the best I can hope for.

Prayer

Almighty God, you made all creatures, even the ones who I can't stand and don't like me. When we clash and step beyond our space, keep me grounded. Let me not lose myself in anger, hate, and disgust. Keep me mindful that all are your children and loved by you. Help me stand in my space and not recklessly give in nor carelessly act out. Guide me so I may be clear about who I am and what I want and need. Amen.

Prompt

When are you good about keeping personal boundaries and when are you not?

sixteen

SELF-CONFIDENCE

*Do not, therefore, abandon that confidence of yours;
it brings a great reward.*
Hebrews 10:35

WHEN I WAS A COLLEGE freshman, I struggled as a writer. I always enjoyed writing. As a boy, I started to pen poetry, but the red ink strewn across my college papers told another story. My professor's criticism tattered my confidence. I hit bottom one late fall day and sat in a secluded spot in the shadow of the tall stone chapel and cried. I didn't know if I could write a proper sentence anymore. Despite my apparent lack of skill, I resolved I would face my problem, not run from it. Whatever the cost might be, I would major in English with a focus on poetry.

At the time, I didn't think my determination came from trust in God. Today, I sense it does. Sitting on those cold steps, I had nothing else. When the storm of life lashes at me, my faith carries me through. From then on I started to sew my writer's confidence back together. I patched it with threads of faith. The repair has taken years, working closely with skilled editors.

In *The Book of Her Life*, the mystic and founder of the Discalced Carmelite movement, Teresa of Avila, advised her novices in the way of prayer and devotion to God. In the thirteenth chapter, she instructs her beginners to "have great confidence, for it is necessary not to hold back one's desires, but to believe in God that if we try we shall little by little, even though it may not be soon, reach the state the saints did with His help."[16] Teresa understood that confidence grows not in giant bounds but in the small, careful steps, little successes that stitch close the wounds of failure.

Our mental health is much like any assault on our confidence. Through small achievements, we can build our determination to risk again. An hour without anxiety or successful self-talk that calms us down is success. These and other wins resurrect what we lost. Knowing that under all the failures is a loving God who raises us is crucial as well.

Prayer

O Lord of redemption and grace, come to my aid when I fail. The pain of failure stings, and my mouth is bitter from the loss and frustration. Rescue me from the mire and lift me up again. With small steps, I can make my way if you show me the path. With your help, I can reach wholeness and health in body and mind. I am expectant and hopeful that your guidance will uphold me and fill me with joy. Amen.

Prompt

What small steps can you make today to grow your confidence?

_____

_____

_____

seventeen

REST

He restoreth my soul.
Psalm 23:2

SLOWING DOWN AND STOPPING TO rest are not things I enjoy doing. Don't get me wrong. When I was a teenager, I could challenge a sloth to a slow-walk race. Not surprisingly, after we had kids, rest was not readily available, but I didn't seek it either. I thought I knew why, but I was wrong.

Rest doesn't just allow the body to recoup. It also gives the mind time to think, and for me, that is the problem. I'm not the only one who struggles with this. Just read the book of Psalms. The great king of Israel, David, wrote many of the poems/prayers called psalms. I can imagine him writing by candlelight in the late-night quiet, lamenting to God all his problems. In Psalm 27 he begins with a question: "The Lord is my light and salvation; whom shall I fear?" He clearly does fear someone because, in the next verse, he writes, "When evildoers assail me to devour my flesh." That verse is full of raw emotion.

After a busy day that hadn't gone well, David poured his heart out to the Lord. He wanted to sleep, but his mind wouldn't stop. Anger, frustration, and fear roiled in him. This happens to me too. I want to sleep, but my mind keeps focusing on the bad stuff: the critical words someone said about my work, attempts to publicly shame me, or threats to undercut me. So I lay awake and relive it all, thinking of better outcomes and wishing I'd reacted better or at all.

So why rest? If I keep going, I'll be too exhausted to think. I can avoid rumination and agitation. But I also don't restore my soul. My body can hack it—at least that's what I thought. We all need the true rest that restores our souls, which means we must stop and allow our mind time. I don't like the ugly feelings that often emerge: frustration, rage, and hatred. They frighten and shame me. I don't want to feel that way, but for God to restore me, I must feel. For many, rest is the only time when the deepest feelings of the soul can arise. That's why you and I need rest.

Prayer

Merciful and kind God, you brought order out of nothing and set the pattern of the world. Help me accept that I need rest, give me assurance that my feelings won't overwhelm me, and care for me when my emotions rise up because I fear my feelings. When sleep won't come and my mind won't stop, grant me patience, knowing that my feelings point to where I need help. I can't do it alone, but with you beside me, I can face my fears. Amen.

Prompt

If you have ever kept busy to avoid your feelings, in what way could God's still waters help you embrace them safely?

_____

_____

_____

_____

_____

_____

_____

_____

_____

_____

_____

_____

_____

_____

_____

_____

_____

_____

_____

_____

eighteen

SABBATH

*Then he said to them, "The sabbath was made for
humankind, and not humankind for the sabbath."*
Mark 2:27

I HAVE A CONFESSION TO make. I often go to the grocery store on
my way home from Sunday services. I'm in my clericals, decked
out in black clothes and a white collar. When I'm tired, I pull up
my jacket zipper to hide my collar so people won't stare, but when
I'm not, I walk through the doors into the fresh produce section
like I'm processing down the church aisle. Some people give me an
odd look. I can't decide—is it their guilt for missing church, again,
or surprise that I'm in a store on the Sabbath?

In the book of Exodus, God told Moses the Israelites were to
keep the Sabbath hallowed (Exodus 20:8). Jesus, however, reframed
it. The Sabbath is meant for our rest, enjoyment, and church too!
But these days, taking a whole day to rest strikes me as extravagant.
No homework, chores, shopping, or getting ready for the week
seems impossible. Instead I tend to compromise. I take a long nap,

watch a game or movie on the couch, tend to my hops, potatoes, or flowers in the garden, go on a walk with my wife, or practice quiet prayer. This is Sabbath for me. If it was made for my rest and enjoyment, then I should rest and enjoy it. For me, even though I work at church, I can do rest too. Praising God, who created the beauty of the hills and valleys, mountains and plains, seaside and forest, is rest and enjoyment.

Young parents often admit to me their struggle taking the Sabbath. My heart breaks when I hear that they can't rest, even for an afternoon. What saddens me more is to discover one of them must work on Sundays, taking an extra shift or job to pay the bills. Researchers have identified that rest, prayer, and even church heals our DNA. It's that important.

God created the Sabbath for us. That tells us something about God. Only a God of love would create a day of rest for us. That's lovely, and when I take Sabbath, I can also feel God's love.

Prayer

O Lord of the day, night, and seasons, you give our lives order and patterns by which to live and call us to rest and relax to restore our bodies, quiet our minds, and heal our souls. Move me to cease my work and trust that I will have enough even though I pause, and let me value the Sabbath not as a rule but as a gift by which I am made whole. In your Son's name I pray. Amen.

Prompt

If you could pause for the gift of the Sabbath, what things do you fear you will miss?

---

nineteen

SLEEP

In the second year of Nebuchadnezzar's reign,
Nebuchadnezzar dreamed such dreams that his spirit
was troubled, and his sleep left him.
Daniel 2:1

LIKE THE BABYLONIAN KING FROM long ago, I have days when I wake up exhausted. Sleep can be the most tiring part of my day. My dreams can be vivid, sometimes because of the meds I'm taking, but other times my brain needs no encouragement. I've had friends, foes, and relatives in my dreams. I am aware that some people enjoy interpreting dreams and even attend seminars and workshops on it, but not me. My dreams are mysterious and draining, and spending more time on them would do me little good.

Despite all the wearying work my brain does at night, sleep is good. I used to stay awake late into the night, not wanting to miss something, but now I go to sleep earlier, looking forward to the morning when I can write in the early light of day. I'm not one to cut my nightly slumber short, ever.

Not everyone would agree with me. In the 1990s I heard a corporate speaker announce that he relished getting four hours of sleep a night. Back then some even argued that less sleep has health benefits and allows people to be more productive. That's rubbish. A few hours' sleep only makes a commuter a danger to self and others. A full night's sleep allows me to think clearly with more creativity. May I have more please?

Like many, on nights when I can't sleep, I often brood over my failures and slights and abuses that were done to me. Those dark thoughts leave me without shut-eye. I hate to admit this, but part of me enjoys stewing over those wrongs, imagining justice being hammered out, but to what end? Once I come to my senses, I do the thing that coaxes me to sleep. I pray. Over the years, I've memorized certain prayers, like the Lord's Prayer, the Prayer of St. Francis, the Twenty-Third Psalm, and the Serenity Prayer. They help quiet my mind and let sleep return.

Prayer

O God, for whom even the darkest night is the noonday, assuage my spirit when I can't sleep and soothe my mind when terror and upheaval seep into my dreams. Keep me from brooding over what has passed. Permit me solace when I lie down and usher in a quiet sleep with pleasant dreams. I seek deep rest and a full night's sleep to strengthen me for the delights and obstacles of a new day. May I rest in the sweetness of your tenderness and under the watchful eyes of the angels. Amen.

Prompt

What are the bad memories that you secretly enjoy but would like to forget?

_____

_____

_____

_____

_____

_____

_____

_____

_____

_____

_____

_____

_____

_____

_____

_____

_____

_____

twenty

SILENCE

Be still, and know that I am God!
Psalm 46:10

IN *SILENCE: A USER'S GUIDE*, the Anglican solitary Maggie Ross observes, "The present age has an ambiguous relationship with silence."[17] She also rightly notes that most dictionary definitions define the word in terms of what it is not, meaning in the negative. When I considered her statement, I tried to express the word affirmatively. I struggled. Ross settled on the biblical term of *beholding*. For me, that word relies too much on sight. I prefer "be-stilling."

These days, I crave silence. I enjoy it because it brings me peace. It re-centers and reconnects me to the great silence of the universe. Silence is the canvas on which God cast the universe and our world. When I am be-still, I can perceive the primordial energy that flows within me and all created things. I find it most in water, which be-stilling is its preferred state. The great Hudson River carries itself as if it was still, though it is not. An undisturbed lake on a windless night is be-stilled. In the Twenty-Third Psalm, the Lord leads the psalmist beside the still waters.

Silence pleases me so because by it I encounter God, or more correctly, I perceive the divine that is already present to me. Ross states that silence brings us "toward the reality and beauty of darkness, unknowing, and beholding that enables the person to receive life afresh, newly created in each moment."[18] Silence fills us, and with our souls filled and opened, we see, hear, and feel the movements of creation and the cries of our neighbors and strangers. Ross again affirms, "In the silence the heart will be changed so that compassion and detachment may arise."[19]

It took work for my journey to silence. In therapy, I expressed my deepest fears and the traumatic events I hid from myself. I now enjoy silence because I no longer fear what swims in the recesses of my mind and memories. I became truly comfortable with myself and discovered the peace that be-stilling can offer. I found God's presence again and again.

Prayer

God of all that lives and moves, call me to be still. Move me from the busyness of my day and draw me beside the still waters, where I can hear you speaking to my soul. Allow me to wade into the dark, inviting waters of calmness and peace. Pull me along gently, and let me be still and sense your presence around me. Amen.

Prompt

What would it feel like to be-stilling?

twenty-one

ASKING FOR HELP

Jethro said to Moses, "What you are doing is not good. You will surely wear yourself out, both you and these people with you. For the task is too heavy for you; you cannot do it alone."
Exodus 18:17–18

I'M A BIT LIKE MOSES, the first leader of the Israelites. I don't like to ask for help. I have my reasons—mostly it shows weakness and makes me feel inadequate. Aren't I supposed to do my share? When I don't, people may think less of me. All of which points to my pride. When I read Jethro's criticism of his son-in-law Moses, I see a proud person not wanting to acknowledge his limits. While he complained about his work, Moses didn't share his duties either, not until his father-in-law intervened. I get why Moses tried to do it all himself. It feels good to be needed and important.

Recognizing when to ask for help is real spiritual maturity. The values of the spiritual life include humility and patience. They speak to another benefit—self-control. Pride steps in front of this, and when it does, trouble is not far behind.

I once had a poor job review because I wasn't communicating what I was doing. In part, I did so because I secretly thought I was better than those around me. I was the expert of all things spiritual and didn't need assistance from people with less expertise. They would mess things up and slow me down. Nice thinking, huh? In the end, I was not showing spiritual maturity, and I am a priest. The shame!

Asking for help is not a weakness. Instead assistance allows both the helper and the helped to grow. Yes, it shows vulnerability, but more importantly, it invites partnership. Jethro told Moses to ask trustworthy people to help him. Like Moses, I've learned to be discerning about who I ask for help, but I ask for help. After that poor review, I teamed up with several people, and they enthusiastically lent a hand. My work improved, and I made a couple of good friends too.

Prayer

Patient and persistent God, turn me from stubbornness and pride. I can be blind and coldhearted and am often in need of your reproving correction. Open my eyes to when I must seek the assistance of others, and soften my heart to those who step forward to help me. Let me grow in patience, humility, and self-control so I may amend my life and better love those around me. Amen.

Prompt

In what ways do you resist help from others? And why?

_____

_____

_____

twenty-two

VULNERABLE

*When the woman saw that she could not remain
hidden, she came trembling; and falling down before
him, she declared in the presence of all the people
why she had touched him, and how she had been
immediately healed.*
Luke 8:47

I RESISTED MEETING MY MOST recent psychiatrist. Don't get me
wrong—I like him. He is professional and listens well. The re-
ligion thing can throw off some in the field of psychiatry, but not
this guy—he gets me. Instead I didn't want to be vulnerable again.
I thought I was getting better and thus could overcome the pro-
longed anxiety without professional help. That was not to be.

My first meeting reminded me of the hemorrhaging woman.
She speaks to the desperation of conditions like anxiety, depression, and suicidal thoughts. Like her, I had to be vulnerable. As
the biblical scholar Frances Taylor Gench writes, "She comes out
of hiding, breaks her silence, and finds her voice; she 'told him the
whole truth.'"[20] At least I can discreetly walk into a nondescript

building to meet my psychiatrist. If an acquaintance saw me, they wouldn't know for sure where I was going. The woman had to be vulnerable with Jesus in public. She trembled and fell down before him because of it.

Jesus's response made all the difference. He said, "Daughter, your faith has made you well; go in peace." As I shared my predicament with my doctor, I wondered if he would dismiss or diminish my feelings or wave off my anxiety. While taking notes, he listened intently and then responded with professional concern. When I think about Jesus's response, I see myself there too. My faith in my new doctor began to make me well. After each visit, I went in peace.

I've been careful with whom I've shared my experiences. After twenty years of living with anxiety, only now am I comfortable enough to write about them publicly. I'm not sharing a secret, rather writing to help you and others. If someone judges me negatively because of the anxiety, depression, or suicidal thoughts, well, there is a special place in hell for them. I'm a priest, after all, and I can say that.

Prayer

Compassionate and healing Lord, you bring us into the light to be healed and dwell in peace. Be kind and generous with me as I open myself to others and you. Deal graciously and tenderly with me as I step timidly toward you. Do not judge me but recognize my faith and honor me for however far I've come. My anxiety and depression and my fearful thoughts of suicide have held me back for so long. I feel unworthy but trust in you. Hear this prayer, O God. Amen.

Prompt

If you could open yourself completely to God, what would you say?

_____

_____

_____

_____

_____

_____

_____

_____

_____

_____

_____

_____

_____

_____

_____

_____

_____

_____

_____

_____

twenty-three

FORGIVENESS

Cast all your anxiety on him,
because he cares for you.
1 Peter 5:7

IT'S NOT YOUR FAULT. FOUR words that change everything. When I realized my body's reaction to fear—the amygdala kidnapping of my emotional and nervous systems—I could forgive myself. Although, it was not easy. The Anglican former archbishop of South Africa Desmond Tutu writes, "Forgiveness is not facile or cheap. It's costly business that makes those who are willing to forgive even more extraordinary."[21] Through forgiveness I could see that my fear, which had invaded my life so often, is a normal reaction.

I've discovered better ways to react to stress than a wild amygdala freaking out, but it took time. I needed to recognize I was afraid of being afraid. What a mess. For starters, I couldn't figure out why my anxiety would start, and then my amygdala shot me down a set of emotional rapids without a paddle. I would careen my way through waves of adrenaline and shuddered at each rise and fall of my heartbeat. I was unable to reach the shore's safety.

With the help of my therapist and calm reflection, I started to recognize my mind's fear. As I calmed my nervous system, I saw I had brought on most of my trouble and then decided it was not fair. When fear is the only reaction available to cope with stress, then fear is the only way I can react. I entered a whirlpool of anxiousness through no fault of my own. Once I knew that, I immediately lamented about the lost and wasted time—years of my life, really. But again, that is not fair.

Forgiveness starts with the self, and thus, as Bishop Tutu wrote, it's "not cheap."[22] When I learned I could make better emotional choices, I grieved about what I'd missed: *If only had I made different choice, what a different person I could be. How many more things could I have done? How much happier would I have been?* Those thoughts hurt, and the only way to make peace with them is through forgiveness.

Remember, it's not your fault either.

Prayer

God of grace, mercy, and forgiveness, I have been afraid and have squandered my time. My emotions have confounded me, and I have grievously misidentified my fears. Relieve me of my worries and concerns; help me recognize the difference between real and false dangers; grant me courage to examine my thoughts and forgive myself where I must. Amen.

Prompt

What are some of the things you can forgive yourself for doing, thinking, or feeling?

twenty-four

SELF-CARE ⚘

And after he had dismissed the crowds, Jesus went up the mountain by himself to pray. When evening came, he was there alone.
Matthew 14:23

A FRIEND ONCE TOLD ME that when I said "maybe," I really meant "no." He was mostly right. My usual response to an invitation I was going to turn down was "maybe," because I didn't like turning people down. I'm getting better, but "no" still feels like I'm disappointing others. For instance, my college friends, who knew me long before I became a priest, like having dinners on Saturday nights. When I get an invite, I often say, "I might come" or "I'll try." But never, "I've got to work Sunday morning. Let's do another night." Besides, these days, I'm not big on dinners. You would think I would tell my friends that, but no. I say "maybe" instead.

Self-care is about doing the little things, like being clear about what I want or need. After a long day helping others, Jesus needed to be by himself and pray. The verse from Matthew shows Jesus's self-care. He sent everyone away so he could be by himself and didn't make a big deal about it. For me, I can take better care of myself by saying "no," not "maybe" or "I'll try." Slowing negative self-talk is another way to care for me. I often can get into "if only" thinking, seeing only my mistakes. Finding the courage to end a toxic relationship is also self-care. I have stayed friends with some people because I felt I should or didn't want to hurt them. Lousy relationships don't help me or anyone else. In the end, who am I helping if I lack candor with myself? I've caused myself a great deal of pain because I lacked the courage to name the obvious.

Self-care is also about integrity. Taking time to feel is a vital part of being honest with myself. As a caregiver, I often put my feelings second or ignore them completely. I can't, however, flourish unless I'm open to my emotions. Just to note, prayer is different than assessing emotions. When I pray, I don't turn my problems over to God. I turn myself over to God. That way I can regain peace, which is the whole point of self-care. Which is why self-care is the first step to thriving.

Prayer

O God of integrity, honesty, and wisdom, I can hide from myself and dismiss my own concerns. Assist me in knowing myself better, letting my feelings emerge, and having the courage to state my needs to myself and others. Give me the confidence to be who I am, not what others want me to be. Let me accept my limits and see myself as worthy of care. Help me trust that others will not reject me when I need to tend to myself. In Jesus's name I pray. Amen.

Prompt

If you could accept your limits better, how would you take care of yourself more?

_____

_____

_____

_____

_____

_____

_____

_____

_____

_____

_____

_____

_____

_____

_____

_____

_____

_____

twenty-five

SELF-KINDNESS

You shall love your neighbor as yourself.
Matthew 19:19

DON'T GET ME WRONG. I love Jesus. Some of his statements, however, are tough. For example, take "love your neighbor as yourself." What he said is simple enough, but what if I don't? I mean, I have days when I don't love myself. I doubt Jesus wants me to lower my ability to love others to match my mood.

What do those days look like when I don't love myself? When I was at my fattest, I didn't love myself. When I had a poor job review, yup, not much love then either. On the day I was turned down for a job, I wasn't full of self-love. I also don't connect well with my emotions. In therapy, I've discovered I can bury my feelings to protect myself, and then it causes anxiety. I had to learn to trust my feelings. When it comes to self-love, I was equally disconnected but had to gain self-kindness first.

The heart of self-kindness is self-love. One goes with the other, and they have a fluid, reciprocal relationship. I've often told myself just to get over my anxiety and have been frustrated with my brain's inability to regulate the secretion of cortisol. For a long time, I would ask myself, why won't this stop? My thoughts would then spiral down a dark, negative trail because I couldn't love myself. Talk about a lack of neighborly love.

I've learned to be kind to myself. When I feel anxiety rising in me, I deepen and slow my breathing and tell myself it's okay to feel. Yes, I actually say that aloud as well as silently. I do so with kindness, often gently rubbing my chest right over my heart. I sometimes worry that my body can't contain my emotions. I know better now.

Self-kindness has changed me and allowed me to grow in self-love and love of others. The kindness I give myself lets me accept myself and all the feelings of which I am capable.

Prayer

Merciful and compassionate Shepherd, protect and guide me with your staff. Lead me from the self-criticisms that drag me into turmoil and anxiousness. Hearten and arouse a spirit of gentleness within me. Help me unite with my emotions and know that I have enough room for each of them. They shall not overcome me, but I will hold them, exploring their depth and breadth. In Jesus's name I pray. Amen.

Prompt

If you could feel God's protection and guidance, how would that strengthen you?

---

twenty-six

SELF-GENTLENESS

*The fruit of the Spirit is love, joy, peace, patience,
kindness, generosity, faithfulness, gentleness,
and self-control.*
Galatians 5:22–23

IN HIS THIRTEEN LETTERS, THE apostle Paul gave lots of advice to the churches he founded. His statement about the fruit of the Spirit remains important, especially for those who face anxiety and depression. Of the nine spiritual attributes, gentleness is perhaps the least valued by today's competitive, fast-paced, get-it-now society but is without question vital for those with mental illness.

Self-gentleness moderates the crushing nature of society when it comes to us. Part of me likes what society values; it's an invisible "perfect" me. Frankly, it's a little devil and often is a voice that makes a spot between my shoulder blades tighten. The tiny bastard says, "You're not enough" and "If you could do more, then you would be truly successful." Rude, right? It feeds on limits: hours in the day, to-do lists, and the schedules, among others. I can't shut it up by yelling at it—that would be weird, anyway. I instead must use gentleness.

When the voice whispers, I do two things. I first remember my past. My perfect self wants me to believe I was better yesterday, last year, or two decades ago than I am now. It tries to convince me I am failing now because I am older and slower. The truth, however, is different. Twenty years ago, my wife and I were raising two young children, and I was running my financial service practice while transitioning to the priesthood. I was busy, not better. Thinking about it now, I laugh because I can't compare my old self to today. We are two different people. The argument the perfect me makes is stupid and irrational, but some days, I easily fall for it.

The second thing I do is pause and soothe myself. I moderate the perfect me into the real me. I admit that I created the to-do list and the schedule, and sometimes with the little devil's input, as a setup for failure. I let go of the self-imposed deadlines, knowing that tomorrow or the next week will give me the time to complete them. Self-gentleness allows me to be happy and fulfilled with whatever I get done.

Prayer

Father and Mother of all that lives, you, O God, give me choice about filling my day. If I fall into idleness, let me not criticize myself and accept that a day or two will cause me no harm. If I work without ceasing, assure me that I can handle it for a bit but encourage me to slow my pace. Raise in me the voice of gentleness so I may care for myself as you want me to do. Soothe my brain when it overflows with thoughts, and bring me to still waters. Amen.

Prompt

In what ways can you be gentle with yourself?

twenty-seven

HUMILITY

*When pride comes, then comes disgrace;
but wisdom is with the humble.*
Proverbs 11:2

How many people do we know who are prideful or lack any sense of humility? I know plenty, and some of them are in my profession. Pride often hides our blind spots, those parts of our character that cause us trouble. I like to think I'm a good priest and preacher. As a part of a training program, I asked a few church members to evaluate my work. What they said was tough to hear but was vital work. When I preach without notes or a text, I wander, and people lose interest. Ouch. The first step is admitting we have blind spots, which moves us a step closer to humility.

Humility can be defined as a feeling of insignificance or inferiority. The author of Proverbs says humility is tied to wisdom, and the wise are not inferior. In *The Sayings of Light and Love*, the sixteenth-century Spanish mystic John of the Cross wrote, "The humble are those who hide in their own nothingness and know how to abandon themselves to God."[23] To be humble is to recognize that God is supreme, we're created by God, and without Him, we do not exist.

When the beauty of a sunset or the silvery light of a full moon casting shadows in the forest catches me, I am humbled. Most of the universe is empty and hostile to life. Still, we exist, and so do enchanting roses and lovely daffodils. We live in this wondrous world, and I am humbled by it. When I consider the smallest creature and the most magnificent galaxy, I realize I am nothing. In those moments, I can only place my hope in God.

Humility with wisdom is real power. The author of Proverbs and John of the Cross recognize the power of God. In our time, many often think we must create and manage our lives on our own. Sure, family and friends help, but we carry our lives as a burden and something we must achieve, but that thinking is wrong and prideful. The wise know that God is our ever-present help. With God's help, we can accomplish so much more and feel truly happy.

Prayer

Merciful and gracious God, you conceived the world and even me. Let me see your works all about me and within me; keep me from prideful ways; turn me from disgrace; grant me wisdom to recognize my limits and seek you in humility. Amen.

Prompt

Where is pride a problem in your life? How could you be more humble?

_____

_____

_____

twenty-eight

VULNERABILITY ⚘

*Therefore I am content with weaknesses, insults,
hardships, persecutions, and calamities for the sake of
Christ; for whenever I am weak, then I am strong.*
2 Corinthians 12:10

PAUL'S STATEMENT ABOUT VULNERABILITY IS boastful. He has
no reservations about who he is and what makes him strong.
Weakness makes him strong. He also recognized his vulnerability
led some to insult and persecute him. I like to say that it freaks
people out, especially these days. Anxiety, depression, and suicidal
crises can make many cringe and respond with an awkward silence.
I want to shake them into a reaction but don't.

I have always been careful about sharing my condition. Even
now, in this book, I've shared with you my experiences of anxiety,
depression, and suicidal ideation but have left out some details,
the private pieces that are not necessary. It's not because they're
scandalous—just not needed. So I've maintained that boundary.
We can be vulnerable while remaining appropriate. I also recognize

that some people will try to take advantage of my vulnerabilities. So I find it best not to boast about them as Paul did.

Vulnerability requires courage. When I accepted my ongoing bouts with anxiety, I grew stronger. I could envision myself standing at the edge of a black void of nothingness and shouting, "I am! I exist!" I'm not defined by my weakness nor strengths but rather by my willingness to be both weak and strong. My vulnerability lets me be at peace with my whole self. Since I don't need to be more than I am, I become strong, and my strength comes from recognizing my vulnerabilities.

Vulnerability also necessitates self-reflection. When I look in the mirror, I am proud of the lines and wrinkles etched on my face. As I have become more aware of my past, I probe my memory for patterns of behavior. Often in therapy, I explore areas where I wasn't at my best and then consider ways I continued that action, seeing if it became a habit. Only then can I identify ways to change and become better. Vulnerability can become a strength, as we appreciate ourselves.

Prayer

O Lord, let not my weakness seem like a fault or mistake but rather a place of honesty, integrity, and vulnerability. When others cringe at my vulnerabilities, hearten my spirit. Increase a discerning spirit in me to recognize when I can speak about my illness in safety. Encourage me to shout at the nothingness that I exist despite the calamities that have beset me. When I look at myself, may I do so with pride, knowing each line and wrinkle have been well earned. Amen.

Prompt

If your weaknesses feel like a fault or mistake, how would seeing them as a place of honesty, integrity, and vulnerability change you?

twenty-nine

ANGELS ⚜

And suddenly angels came and waited on Jesus.
Matthew 4:11

I BELIEVE IN ANGELS. THEY'RE in the Bible, and the church has
affirmed their existence, even if today it does so quietly. I'm not
quiet about them. I love them. I can't say that I've seen any, but I
have felt one's presence twice in my life.

During my college sophomore year, I traveled to New York
City with a dormmate and his girlfriend. We took his light-blue
Dodge Dart, and he drove along a busy Connecticut interstate in a
heavy, cold autumn rain. As we neared a toll plaza, the car hit a pot-
hole, and he lost control. Instead of holding the steering wheel, my
dormmate snatched at a pile of napkins flying off the dashboard.
The car whirled between other vehicles, a large dump truck, and a
Greyhound bus. It spun from the far-left lane until it reached the
shoulder on the opposite side. Go figure—not a scratch. We were
even facing the right way. How did that happen? By serendipity or
an angel's hand?

One early October morning, when I was overwhelmed by the thought of suicide, I left my first class and headed to the place where I would end my life. On my way, my soul cried, and several voices answered, saying what I was about to do wasn't right. Not that it was a sin, but just not what I honestly wanted. Suicide is a complex illness of the brain and not an affront to God. Those voices encouraged me to go to the dean of students' office. No doubt I heard the voices of angels.

Angels have specific roles. In the Bible, they announce a change and care for those in need, like Jesus. They still do. During her first rapture, the sixteenth-century Spanish Carmelite nun and mystic Teresa of Avila heard the Lord say, "No longer do I want you to converse with men but with angels." Another time she had felt the presence of angels during a profound and delightful moment of prayer.[24] I believe they guide us to heaven when we die, as well.

We don't control angels and can't demand their presence, but at times, they are with us. It's a blessing to know they exist and can gather around us. So we shouldn't hesitate to ask God to send them our way when we are in need.

Prayer

Generous and merciful God, you created both the visible and the invisible and surround yourself with companies of angels and archangels. I beseech you to grant me the presence of an angel in times of danger and distress. When the darkness of the world assails me, send a holy one to be with me. Let me feel a guardian's presence when my fears overwhelm me. For only by your kindness, am I safe. Amen.

Prompt

If you think back over your life, do you see moments when angels may have been present?

thirty

WORTHINESS ❧

*Look at the birds of the air; they neither sow nor reap
nor gather into barns, and yet your heavenly Father
feeds them. Are you not of more value than they?*
Matthew 6:26

I'VE HAD MY FAIR SHARE of disappointments. I've been denied a promotion and raises. More times than I can count, I have had manuscripts rejected. This one was tough: My wife and I honeymooned in Bermuda for a week. The Tuesday after we returned, my boss met me in the building's coffee shop and told me my job was eliminated. (Later, the unemployment office would say that my employer claimed I was fired for cause, as if!) I took the next train out of New York City and called my wife with the news from the station—she's a champ, right? I was shocked by what had happened. It took me some weeks to figure out what was next, partly because the job loss crushed my self-worth. Refusals, denials, and rejections can hurt deeply.

At the heart of worthiness is the story we tell ourselves. Most of us have a narrative about our lives, a story about the way we should live. Our family influences it. Statements like, "When are you going to have children?" which both our mothers asked. The culture also affects the story. Advertisements, school, and social media shape the way we think, trying to get us to buy certain products that meet a perceived storyline. We have our dreams. Each of these creates a set of expectations, and when we fail to reach them, our self-worth often suffers.

Our narrative, however, doesn't include disappointments or rejections. No one dreams about tragedy and loss. That would be dark, but our lives include them. When they happen, what then? For me, I have found help in knowing God doesn't make junk, rubbish, litter, garbage, or trash. God also doesn't make mistakes. Let that sink in.

Prayer

Almighty and gracious God, you value me more than I know and, at times, more than I do myself. When disappointments, rejection, refusals, and denials ensue, console and reassure me that to you, I am worthy. If I fail to meet my expectations, remind me life does not always unfold the way I want. Make me aware of the influence of others that skew my hopes and dreams. If tragedy happens, revive in me your vision for my life. In Jesus's name I pray. Amen.

Prompt

How does knowing God values you more than you do yourself change your outlook?

thirty-one

WISDOM

*For wisdom is better than jewels, and all that you
may desire cannot compare with her.*
Proverbs 8:11

IN THE BOOK OF PROVERBS, the figure of wisdom is a woman who teaches the willing how to live a good life, acting the right way toward oneself and others. Central to wisdom is learning, which often goes unheeded. For example, "Wisdom cries out in the street; in the squares she raises her voice" (1:20). In my experience with mental illness, the advice given by psychiatrists and therapists is valuable, but at times, the wisdom they impart is incomplete.

Wisdom isn't only taught—it must be earned. Time and experience matter as much as understanding. I can understand the way the brain and nervous system react to perceived or real fear; however, that knowledge did not halt my anxiety. My learning had to be seasoned by the ordeal. I needed to experience anxiety and use different behavioral tools to lessen it. I had to determine that dread was wrong. I would often talk with my wife about what was happening, which helped me evaluate myself. (Did I mention that we've been married since 1989? What a saint!) It's anxiety, not a heart attack, I would say.

Later, wisdom taught me my anxiety was a sign, a smoke signal from my psyche. Wisdom alerted me to what was wrong and showed a path to health. Once I listened to her, I began to unload my burdens in therapy. As the author of Proverbs writes, "Those who listen to me [wisdom] will be secure and will live at ease, without dread of disaster" (Proverbs 1:33). Wisdom's teachings, the signposts to health, can ease anxiousness.

The Christian tradition teaches that God is three persons, like a three-leaf clover: one plant but three parts. (A friend once taught me that.) In *Showings*, Julian of Norwich, who in addition to being a mystic was an anchoress, wrote, "God almighty is our loving father, and God all wisdom is our loving Mother, with the love and the goodness of the Holy Spirit, which is all one God, one Lord."[25] Wisdom is the best part of a mother, who teaches us the way to thrive.

Prayer

O holy Wisdom, your guidance shows me the way to thrive. Instill in my heart such knowledge of you that I love all that you teach. Imbue in me a spirit of curiosity and desire for the way to a good life. Open my eyes to the right path, and gently stir my thoughts toward right living. With time and wise counsel, let me see that your guidance and instruction will lead me to joy, peace, and hope. In your name I pray. Amen.

Prompt

Through what experiences have you earned wisdom?

_____

_____

thirty-two

GRATEFULNESS ⤳

*Then Naomi said to her daughter-in-law [Ruth],
"Blessed be he by the Lord, whose kindness has not
forsaken the living or the dead!"*
Ruth 2:20

THE SUICIDE-PREVENTION FUNDRAISER HAD JUST ended, and my wife and I were flush with the gathering's friendly warmth but also moved by the bittersweet tributes to those who had died by suicide. I turned to her and said, "I am grateful that I didn't end my life." As I said it, I had a revelation. Although ten years had passed since the day I was in a suicidal crisis, I was only then able to express profound gratefulness. I needed time and to hear others' pain before I could feel grateful for living. The suicidal crisis is utterly life altering.

Like Naomi, my gratefulness emerged in the recovery after a tragedy. I needed to feel safe, realizing the threat of suicide had finally faded. In the muck and mire of anxiety and depression, I hardly felt grateful. I could appreciate a beautiful day and the kindness of my wife and children, but I didn't have abiding gratitude for being alive. The adrenaline and other chemicals continued to flow from my brain into my body, limiting me to the immediacy of the struggle.

Without the courage to live, however, I wouldn't have found gratefulness. Small steps and little daily victories led me back to gratefulness. I still feel as if I am a veteran of a grizzly battle, not with a distant stare but filled with wisdom seasoned by experience. I am grateful to have returned to wholeness, to thrive again, and for whom I have become. I don't value the suffering and don't wish it upon others. I have been forged, hardened, tempered, and refined on the anvil of God.

Ruth's decision to stay with Naomi let her mother-in-law be among the living, not the dead. Ruth brought Naomi into a new family that gave her safety and security. Her deep and abiding gratefulness came from knowing she would not dwell in despair but live in goodness. She would thrive again.

Prayer

Lord of hopefulness and God of grace, I thank you for the life I live. It has not unfolded as I had hoped or imagined, but I am better for it. I have suffered but endured, been in darkness but found the light, and stumbled blindly but can see once again. Lead me, O God, to a place where I can thrive, being fully myself and all you hope I can become. In your name I pray. Amen.

Prompt

What are you grateful for, and what does thriving mean to you?

thirty-three

LETTING GO ⚘

Look at the birds of the air; they neither sow nor reap
nor gather into barns, and yet your heavenly Father
feeds them. Are you not of more value than they?
Matthew 6:26

ARE YOU FAMILIAR WITH A trust fall? It's supposed to be a simple team-building activity. A person stands a few feet above others with her back turned. After folding her arms across her chest, she falls backward into the waiting arms below. I was once asked to do it blindfolded, and with my unexamined trust issues, I couldn't let go and trust others to catch me. So I kind of squatted down, and the group awkwardly supported me into their arms.

When anxiety has hold of me, letting go is not simple or easy. A battle breaks out in my brain between my rational self, or frontal cortex, and the chemicals secreting from the almond-shaped neurons called the amygdala. The amygdala usually wins, and my heartbeat rapidly quickens. With the help of my therapist, I have lessened my fear and the worry that sets off anxiety. It often involves giving me a break. But there is more to life, a deeper way to be.

I become most relaxed when I let go, not just of fear and worry, but everything, even life itself. I become detached from everything. In *The Book of the Perfect Life*, an anonymously written fourteenth-century Germanic text, the author states that when a person becomes detached, one is "free of will, love, desire, knowledge, and so on," and "the less one lays claim to these, the nobler, pure, and more godly they become."[26] When I release my mind and go into the loving abyss of the divine, I realize that I am nothing and yet cherished by God.

Whatever its source, anxiety's grip is unyielding. We can endure the chemical reaction with the help of meds. I have done so for years. But I want to float away with God, even if my heart still beats quickly and the amygdala's secretions haven't stopped. But I am no longer held hostage by them. Anxiety happens in the body but not in my soul. When I recognize I am not the anxiety, fear, or worry, I become something more. I am a cherished soul that is embodied to engage the world, which can be harsh and unrelenting.

Prayer

O God, you mingle between the strands of my DNA and in the silence between my heartbeats. Open my eyes to see you in my life and remind me that while my body may be ill and one day will die, my soul lives forever. Help me let go of the things that push against me, and free me from the clutches of fear and worry that I harbor. Guide me to that gentle place where you caress me. Amen.

Prompt

What would it feel like to completely let go?

thirty-four

STRENGTH ✣

He gives power to the faint
and strengthens the powerless.
Isaiah 40:29

I COACHED MIDDLE SCHOOL AND high school athletes for ten
seasons. One thing I learned and then taught is athletes do not
know their own strength. They don't know how much their bodies
can handle. When athletes feel discomfort, many become fearful
and back off. What they need in those moments is the watchful eye
of an experienced coach who can help them go further. A responsi-
ble coach is mindful of pain and improper technique that can lead
to injuries, but that aside, athletes need coaches to encourage them
to achieve greater heights.

Like a coach, God can encourage us to go further than we
can imagine. The renowned nineteenth-century preacher Phillips
Brooks once wrote that for some, especially the young, God is "the
Setter of great tasks; the God who holds His crown of victory on
the tops of high mountains."[27] God's goal setting is for all, not just
the young.

When God called me to the priesthood, I merely wanted to help people through life transitions. I thought I could do that best by serving high school students. After being a high school chaplain for a few years, I sensed I was better suited elsewhere. I enjoyed teaching, coaching, and ministering to teenagers but recognized I needed a different challenge, a more significant task. I soon began my doctoral studies—something I hadn't considered when I was young. I also started working with churches in transition between long-serving pastors. It can be stressful work, but I'm good at it. I began teaching master-level students at a seminary. Before seminary, I didn't imagine doing any of this.

God strengthens you and me. With God's encouragement, we can achieve much more than we think. The power and strength I received and continue to receive are available to everyone. I'm not talking about blind faith, but thoughtful trust that allows us to grow under the watchful eye of our loving God.

Prayer

O God, you inspire people to great tasks and stir imaginations to strive after the unimaginable. Strengthen me to take on challenges and overcome the obstacles in my life. Be a beacon of encouragement, leading me down untrodden paths and to hold high the standard of greatness you have for me. Build up my spirit to keep on when others doubt, and increase my trust in you. Amen.

Prompt

In what ways could you trust God more?

_____

_____

_____

_____

_____

_____

_____

_____

_____

_____

_____

_____

_____

_____

_____

_____

_____

_____

_____

_____

_____

thirty-five

LOVE, LIFE, AND GOD

> *Let him kiss me with the kisses of his mouth!*
> *For your love is better than wine,*
> *your anointing oils are fragrant,*
> *your name is perfume poured out;*
> *therefore the maidens love you.*
> Song of Solomon 1:2–3

LIKE MANY PEOPLE, MY LIFE has been filled with despair, pain, anxiety, depression, anguish, and mourning, but even so, I love life. I enjoy the warmth of a sunny afternoon, the quiet songs of a bird, and the stirring of a gentle breeze that are typical beauties of my surroundings. I also find pleasure in conversations with friends and strangers that point to hope and grace. Even after having kissed the dead and holding the hand of the dying, I still love life. I appreciate all facets of life.

As the maiden exclaims in the opening verses of the Hebrew poem Song of Solomon I too love God both spiritually and physically. Why shouldn't I? I am married to my best friend and dearest love, but I still love the one who created me. My affection is more than I have for a parent. I am attracted to God in a physically and spiritually sensual way. When I enter a church sanctuary on a quiet afternoon to pray, my passion for God fills me. When I walk outdoors, smelling the pungent aroma of life, I am overcome with desire for the Creator. Whether it's in a holy place set aside by humans or the cathedral of nature, I can feel God and am in love with God and life.

Love can be expressed many ways. For example, John of the Cross writes about the fire of love. God can give a soul "some secret touches of love that pierce and wound it like fiery arrows, leaving it wholly cauterized by the fire of love."[28] The soul with wounds of love burns itself anew. Having burned off the accretions of self-centeredness, God brings the wounded soul to nothing, "knowing nothing save love."[29] We are meant for nothing more in this world than to love life and God. By this love, we have the courage to do anything, and by it, we thrive.

Prayer

My lover and the creator of life, you, O God, give me the passion and desire for all things. You have blessed me with many ways and places where we can be intimate. My heart and soul warm and long for our secluded moments of passion. Draw me away to your playful gardens growing with the nectar of your creation. Pull me close so I may smell your aroma and feel your breath. I am grateful for life and you. Amen.

Prompt

If you could tell a friend about your love of God, what would you say?

thirty-six

PATIENCE

May you be made strong with all the strength that comes from his glorious power, and may you be prepared to endure everything with patience.
Colossians 1:11

WHEN MY HEART FIRST STARTED pounding and beating rapidly in the middle of the night, I could do little to stop what was happening. Sometimes the medicine worked, and other times, not so much. I would either lie in bed or watch television. Prayer and relaxed breathing helped a bit, but after many years of these anxiety attacks, I've learned that I needed to endure them patiently.

Patience didn't come easily. It was earned. Tears often moistened my pillow while I silently waited for my brain to let go. I'm the person who would rather dart to my car in a thunderstorm than wait for it to pass. But unlike a storm, there was no place of safety nor shelter from the stormy blast, as the old church hymn goes.

Once my doctors assured me that these "events" weren't going to kill me, I was able to let go of the dread and wait patiently, resting in the folds of God's arms. Eventually, my heart would ease back into a normal rhythm, and I drifted off to sleep.

The next day was always rough. Groggy and off kilter, I went to the church office, with my best smile painted on my face, and I had to. I didn't want my parishioners to know. Some wouldn't resist checking on me, and I didn't want to hear, "Gee, Father, you look like hell today." My wife, my fearless supporter, got me, but I didn't want to worry my kids. I can explain an illness easily, but brain chemistry and anxiety are different, don't you think?

After many years and lots of therapy, I found a path out of the storm. What helps me most is a patient understanding of what I can and can't control. Of course, we can't control other or the brain. Only after patiently examining and recasting the trauma in my life was I able to find peace. That wisdom is hard won through patience.

Prayer

Blessed and mighty Lord, you established the world and keep its course. Come to my aid when the storm of anxiety besets upon me. Hold me in the fold of your arms while my heart shudders and my body trembles. Grant me the knowledge that I will not pass into the abyss and the patience to weather the blast of fear from my unspoken traumas. Assist me in shining a light on what makes me afraid and being my companion as I endure the tumult of my mind, in Jesus's name I pray. Amen.

Prompt

What are some of the things you fear most?

thirty-seven

JOY ❧

You show me the path of life. In your presence there is
fullness of joy; in your right hand are pleasures
for evermore.
Psalm 16:11

O N A RECENT WALK, MY wife and I spoke about joy. She said
it's different than happiness. Joy is deeper. While she might
feel happy on a particularly lovely day, joy comes through her relationships with friends, especially when laughing and remembering
good times. Happiness is an emotion that lasts a short while; joy is
a state of being.

In the Bible, joy is expressed both in the Hebrew and Christian
Scriptures. A marriage, the birth of a child, a successful harvest are
reasons for joy. God's actions on behalf of Israel are also reasons for
joy. Even when a foreign power oppressed them, they felt joy as
anticipatory of God's rescue, especially at the end of the ages. For
Christians, Jesus's birth and resurrection were reasons for the highest state of joy. Notice how it flows from relationships with others
or God. My wife, of course, was right.

When depression hung over me like cold shade, joy was far removed. I lived each day with lots of emotions but felt distanced from the pleasure I had felt so strongly when God first called me to the priesthood. At that time, joy overflowed in me. I sometimes thought I would burst because of it. I once sent a joyful email to a group of friends; some of them felt it was too saccharine. Oh well! But during my first year of seminary, I had no joy, and I felt cut off or muted.

Joy emerges from the soul. Like a plucked string, it resonates with the strings in others' souls. This is why the Bible associates joy with marriage, births, and productive harvests. It involves connecting with others, the world, and God. The soul sings with joy when it lets go and is unconcerned about anything at all—spiritual emptiness at its highest. Joy is unabashed, unbashful, unfettered bonding with others.

Prayer

O delightful and joyful God, with you my soul sings with love and bliss. Send forth your sweet perfumes and pleasant songs to fill me to the brim. Let my spirit wash over in ecstasy and peace. Stir my heart with your cheer, and pour in your elixirs of grace and goodness. Grant me your treasures of love, faith, and hope. I give you all my love, O blessed God of happiness. Amen.

Prompt

If you could live one day filled with joy, what would that be like?

_____

_____

_____

thirty-eight

PEACE

*Peace I leave with you; my peace I give to you. I do
not give to you as the world gives. Do not let your
hearts be troubled, and do not let them be afraid.*
John 14:27

FOR A TIME, MY ANXIETY wouldn't leave me, a kind of low-level disturbance in my body that caused an irregular heartbeat. When it happened a second time, however, it didn't upset me like before. I didn't have the looming dread that came with the first wave of panic attacks. There was another reason.

I could dwell in spiritual peace. While I couldn't control my nervous system or my amygdala or the chemical reactions of my brain, I could choose how I reacted. Although my body followed my brain's signals, I didn't freak out. I could close my eyes and check on my soul and discover it was fine.

The soul is different than the body. The fourth-century north-African Christian theologian and mystic Augustine of Hippo explained that the soul has "an essence all its own" and "its homeland, is God Himself by whom it has been created."[30] In the *Care of the Soul*, the twentieth-century American psychotherapist and former monk Thomas Moore writes, "'Soul' is not a thing, but a quality or a dimension of experiencing life and ourselves. It has to do with depth, value, relatedness, heart, and personal substance."[31] We can, therefore, evaluate the soul independently from the body. While we can't fully understand the soul, we can be aware of and intimately harmonize with it.

When I am caught up with anxiety, I can be at peace. In my soul, my core and essence, I am not disturbed. Even so, I didn't want to suffer from anxiety endlessly, which is why I sought therapy. I needed a professional's guidance to uncover the root of my troubles. At first treatment didn't help my heartbeat return to normal, but I remained committed. When I finally identified the multilayered origins of the upheavals, my soul's peace didn't change—the anxiety did.

Prayer

O God, the greatest gift your Son Jesus left us was peace. It is our compass through anxiety's onslaught, the map through the murkiness of depression, the lighthouse's beam in the throes of suicidal crisis. Let your peace flow from my soul to keep me calm and grounded even when life is at its worst. Through it all, I am ever your possession, and you are my shelter, whom I ever love. In Jesus's name I pray. Amen.

Prompt

If you could draw a picture of a time when you were at peace, what would it look like?

thirty-nine

HOPE

*And hope does not disappoint us, because God's love
has been poured into our hearts through the Holy
Spirit that has been given to us.*
Romans 5:5

IN MY CLASHES WITH ANXIETY, depression, panic, and suicidal thoughts, I became frustrated, disappointed, angered, desolate, and desperate, but I kept my hope. In my soul, I remained confident that one day I would overcome the illness in my brain and would heal. Hope allowed me to get out of bed, be with my family, and serve the people entrusted to my care. Hope also allowed me to laugh and find joy, even in times when my brain said otherwise.

In *The Book of Her Life*, Teresa of Avila wrote, "Once in comforting me He told me with much love that I shouldn't be anxious, that in this life we cannot always be in a stable condition, that sometimes the soul will experience fervor and at other times be without it, that sometimes it will have disturbances and at other times have quiets, and again temptations; but that it should hope in Him and not be afraid."[32] While the late Middle Ages didn't share our understanding of brain chemistry, her reference to the soul's different states is not wrong. In her encounter with God, she learned that humans could have a variety of feelings and emotions and not lose hope. We are meant to have a full range of emotions. It's normal and okay.

Our culture and workweek life can dull our existence. We can fall into habits and patterns that make us exist with little expectation of irregularity. In the dullness of our routines, we can forget we feel and move from one task to the next chore with little emotional engagement. Until one day, the brain says *enough*, or the soul cries *stop*. We are suddenly launched into a swirling pool of emotions. When that happened to me, I felt as if I was drowning, and being unprepared, I panicked. Hope kept me swimming, even when I doubted my strength. Hope didn't disappoint me.

Prayer

O God, you lead and guide me toward the land of hope, where your light and love shine forever. Give me the confidence to feel all my emotions, even the ones that mystify or scare me. Let me not live this day without connecting to the various feelings I may have. I want to unite with all of them so I may thrive, loving each moment I'm alive. In your gracious name I pray. Amen.

Prompt

What would your life be like if you were filled with hope?

forty

THRIVE

They shall again live beneath my shadow,
they shall flourish as a garden;
they shall blossom like the vine,
their fragrance shall be like the wine of Lebanon.
Hosea 14:7

ALL HUMANS WANT TO THRIVE. I can think of no other state that brings me joy, peace, and hope. When I strip my other desires, my soul longs to thrive, and nothing more. I can close my eyes, connect with my soul, and feel it radiating at the thought.

Anxiety, depression, and suicidal thoughts feel far away from thriving. When I would hold myself close during a panic attack, a deep, dark gulf separated me from the place where I can flourish or bloom. I saw no way across, but the state of thriving was not lost or gone forever into the haze of despair.

At first I traversed the gulf with uncertain steps. I had to relearn to trust my body, brain, and emotions. I felt so betrayed by them, which filled me not just with doubt but shame as well. I needed the courage to walk the narrow trail with cliffs falling away on both sides. When I crossed wobbly bridges that spanned the darkness, I needed to be brave. With every step, however, I learned more about myself, accepted my limitations, and came closer to thriving. My confidence returned.

I believe that having read this far, you have the courage to thrive. Perhaps I've been your mentor, and maybe some devotions have mirrored your life. I hope and pray that I've motivated you to follow my journey. By recognizing God's presence in your life, you can take small steps that are, in truth, big steps, finding your way to the state of thriving. After Jesus healed someone, he often said, "Go in peace." He recognized the way humans are at their best: filled with joy, peace, and hope. I don't profess you will miraculously be healed, but rather, through a courageous commitment to travel toward thriving, you can find wholeness where you are no longer a victim to your body, brain, and emotions.

Prayer

Draw near to me, loving God, and hear my petitions. I long to thrive. Grant me the courage to bridge the gulf that separates me from what my soul desires. Embolden me to keep following the well-worn path leading to joy. Send me in peace into the world and its mixture of delights and disappointments. Provide me always with hope that by it, I will remain a grateful and courageous child of yours. Amen.

Prompt

If you could thrive today, what would you do?

_____

_____

ACKNOWLEDGMENTS

THIS BOOK CAME ABOUT IN a Spirit-led conversation with the publisher of Redemption Press, Athena Dean Holtz. I approached her about another book, but as we spoke, *Courage to Thrive* came into being. Only the goodness of the Lord could lead us in such a way. I am grateful to Athena for her willingness to hear the Spirit working and encouraging me to pursue this book.

I have a lifetime of experience with mental health struggles and am grateful to all the therapists and doctors who have helped me along the way. I am most appreciative of my current therapist and my psychiatrist for guiding me through one of the most difficult periods of my life. Because of their professionalism and care, I am the healthiest I have ever been.

I am also grateful to the American Foundation for Suicide Prevention. For ten years I have been blessed to be a volunteer and have come to understand mental health and especially suicide in a profound way. Their work saves lives, and I am happy to help them. I can't overlook Mel Varady, who asked me to join the AFSP a decade ago. She has been a wonderful friend.

I also want to extend my thanks for Cynthia Cavanaugh, Hannah McKenzie, and the terrific team at Redemption Press. Books usually take a year or more to bring to life. We did this one in less than six months. Thank you!

ENDNOTES

1. Dante Alighieri, *Inferno*, vol. 1 of *The Divine Comedy of Dante Alighieri*, ed. and trans. Robert M. Durling (New York: Oxford Univ. Press, 1996), 27.

2. William Styron, *Darkness Visible: A Memoir of Madness* (New York: Vintage Books, Random House, 1992), 83.

3. Alighieri, *Inferno*, 541.

4. Lord Moran, *The Anatomy of Courage: The Classic WWI Account of the Psychological Effects of War* (New Yok: Carroll & Graf, 2007), 67.

5. Lord Moran, *The Anatomy of Courage*, 123.

6. Lord Moran, *The Anatomy of Courage*, xiv.

7. Lord Moran, *The Anatomy of Courage*, 120.

8. Julian of Norwich, *Showings*, trans. Edmund Colledge and James Walsh (Mahwah, NJ: Paulist Press, 1978), 300.

9. Julian of Norwich, *Showings*, 301.

10. St. John of the Cross, *The Collected Works of St. John of the Cross*, trans. Kieran Kavanaugh and Otilio Rodriguez (Washington, DC: Institute of Carmelite Studies, 1991), 243.

11. Julian of Norwich, *Showings*, 225.

12. St. John of the Cross, *The Collected Works of St. John of the Cross*, 296.

13. Scott M. Peck, *The Road Less Traveled: A New Psychology of Love, Traditional Values and Spiritual Growth* (New York: Simon & Schuster, Touchstone, 1978), 3.

14. "Cope," *Online Etymology Dictionary*, https://www.etymon-line.com/search?q=cope, accessed May 30, 2020.

15. Robert Frost, *Poems by Robert Frost: A Boy's Will and North of Boston* (New York: Penguin Books, New American Library, Signet Classic, 1990), 76–77.

16. St. Teresa of Avila. *The Collected Works of St. Teresa of Avila*, 2nd ed., trans. Kieran Kavanaugh and Otilio Rodriguez (Washington, DC: Institute of Carmelite Studies, 1987), 123.

17. Maggie Ross, *Process*, vol. 1 of *Silence: A User's Guide* (Eugene, OR: Wipf & Stock, Cascade Books, 2014), 38.

18. Ross, *Process*, 221.

19. Ross, *Process*, 221.

20. Frances Taylor Gench, *Back to the Well: Women's Encounters with Jesus in the Gospels* (Louisville, KY: Westminster John Knox Press, 2004), 36.

21. Simon Wiesenthal, *The Sunflower: On the Possibilities and Limits of Forgiveness* (New York: Schocken Books, 1998), 267.

22. Simon Wiesenthal, *The Sunflower*, 267.

23. St. John of the Cross, *The Collected Works of St. John of the Cross*, 97.

24. St. Teresa of Avila, *The Collected Works of St. Teresa of Avila*, 211 & 359.

25. Julian of Norwich, *Showings*, 293.

26. *The Book of the Perfect Life,* trans. David Blamires (Walnut Creek, CA: Rowman & Littlefield, AltaMira Press, 2003), 34.

27. Phillips Brooks, *The Consolations of God: Great Sermons of Phillips Brooks*, ed. Ellen Wilbur (Grand Rapids, MI: William B. Eerdmans, 2003), 71.

28. St. John of the Cross, *The Collected Works of St. John of the Cross*, 484.

29. St. John of the Cross, *The Collected Works of St. John of the Cross*, 485.

30. St. Augustine, *The Greatness of the Soul*, trans. Joseph M. Colleran. *Ancient Christian Writers: The Works of the Fathers in Translation*, eds. Johannes Quasten and Joseph C. Plumpe, no. 9 (Mahwah, NJ: Paulist Press, Newman Press, 1978), 14.

31. Thomas Moore, *Care of the Soul: A Guide for Cultivating Depth and Sacredness in Everyday Living* (New York: HarperPerennial, 1994), 5.

32. St. Teresa of Avila. *The Collected Works of St. Teresa of Avila*, 360.

ORDER INFORMATION

REDEMPTION P R E S S

To order additional copies of this book, please visit
www.redemption-press.com.
Also available on Amazon.com and BarnesandNoble.com
or by calling toll-free 1-844-2REDEEM.

CPSIA information can be obtained
at www.ICGtesting.com
Printed in the USA
LVHW041203210920
666634LV00003B/298

9 781646 451777